Science in Ancient Egypt

Geraldine Woods

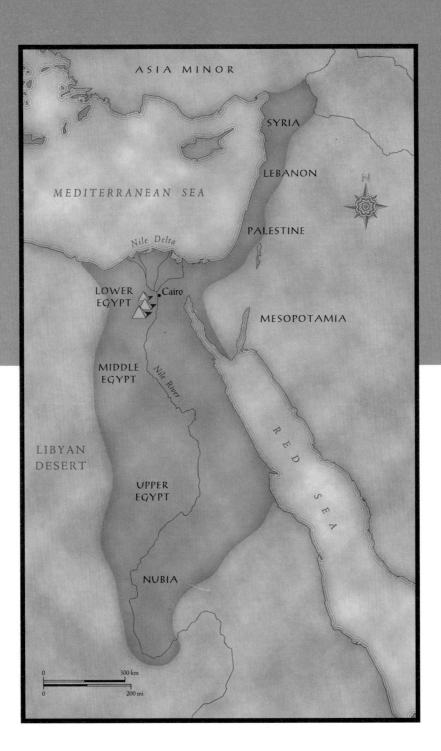

ASIA MINOR

SYRIA

LEBANON

MEDITERRANEAN SEA

PALESTINE

Nile Delta

LOWER
EGYPT

•Cairo

MESOPOTAMIA

MIDDLE
EGYPT

Nile River

LIBYAN
DESERT

RED SEA

UPPER
EGYPT

NUBIA

N

0   300 km
0   200 mi

Science in Ancient Egypt

Geraldine Woods

Science of the Past

FRANKLIN WATTS

A Division of Grolier Publishing
New York • London • Hong Kong • Sydney
Danbury, Connecticut

Visit Franklin Watts on the Internet at: http://publishing.grolier.com

Photographs ©: Ancient Art & Architecture Collection Ltd.: 10 (Mary Jelliffe), 49 (Mary Jelliffe), 6, 30, 44, 45, 46 (Ronald Sheridan), 24 (John P. Stevens); Archive Photos: 17; Art Resource: 52, 55 (Werner Forman Archive, Schimmel Collection, New York); Bendick Association: 58; Boltin Picture Library: 27, 28, 56; Corbis-Bettmann: 9, 26, 31, 47; Erich Lessing/Art Resource: 42, 48 top; Folio, Inc.: 13 (Ira Wexler); Giraudon/Art Resource: 48 bottom; The Metropolitan Museum of Art, Rogers Fund, 1948: 41; Peter Arnold Inc.: 12 (Malcom S. Kirk); Photo Researchers: 11, 25 (Carolyn Brown), 53 (Roemer-Pelizaeus Museum, Hildesheim); Photri: 32; Reuters/Mohamed el-Dakhakhny/Archive Photos: 54; Scala/Art Resource: 15, 51; Superstock, Inc.: cover (Egyptian National Museum, Cairo, Egypt/ET Archive) 7, 40; Tony Stone Images: 50 (Rex A. Butcher), 38 (Charles Thatcher); Visuals Unlimited: 8 (Les Christman).

Map created by XNR Productions Inc.

Illustrations by Drew-Brook-Cormack Associates

Library of Congress Cataloging-in-Publication Data

Woods, Geraldine
    Science in ancient Egypt / Geraldine Woods
    p. cm. (Science of the past)
    Includes bibliographical references and index.
    Summary: Discusses the achievements of the ancient Egyptians in science, mathematics, astronomy, agriculture, and technology.
    ISBN 0-531-20341-7 (lib. bdg.)   0-531-15915-9 (pbk.)
    1. Science—Egypt—History—Juvenile literature. 2. Engineering—Egypt—History—Juvenile literature. 3. Science, Ancient—Juvenile literature. [1. Science—Egypt—History. 2. Technology—Egypt—History. 3. Science, Ancient.] I. Title. II. Series.
Q127.E3W66   1998
509'.32—dc21
                 97-649
                 CIP
                 AC

CONTENTS

chapter 1

Egypt's Debt to the Nile

Ancient Egypt developed along the shores of the Nile River.

The Nile River winds through more than 4,000 miles (6,400 km) of Africa before emptying into the Mediterranean Sea. About 10,000 years ago, the Egyptian civilization began developing along a narrow strip of land on either side of the Nile. Beyond this strip lay vast desert. The Nile made it possible for a great civilization to grow in an area with a dry, harsh climate.

For most of the year, the Nile flows peacefully to the sea. But each summer, when heavy rains fall, the river rises and rises until it floods. Before modern dams were built, the Nile overflowed its banks every year.

The rich soil along the banks of the Nile was ideal for growing grains such as wheat and barley.

The early Egyptians used a *shaduf,* a long pole balanced on a wooden beam with a weight at one end and a bucket at the other. to move water from the canals to the fields.

The floods watered Egyptian farmers' crops and enriched the soil with *silt* from the river.

The earliest farmers had no choice but to wait patiently for the Nile to flood. But then, about 7,000 years ago, the Egyptians invented the world's first irrigation system. They dug canals to direct water from the river to distant fields. Later, the Egyptians began to build reservoirs to hold the water, so that they would have water to use during the dry season.

Besides being among the first societies to grow crops, the Egyptians were also one of the first groups of people to tame animals and breed them for work or food. They raised oxen, cattle, sheep, goats, pigs, and

This mural from a 3,500-year-old tomb shows Egyptans plowing their fields, sowing seeds, and harvesting crops.

donkeys. They kept antelopes, geese, and ducks for meat and collected honey and wax from beehives.

The ancient Egyptians knew how to preserve animal meat by drying it in the sun or salting it. They were the first people to make leather from animal hides. They even brewed beer and wine from the plants they grew. All of this was possible because the Nile supplied the Egyptians with a source of water and fertile land.

The Nile also inspired early Egyptian science. To predict the flooding of the Nile, the Egyptians made a calendar. To measure the flood, they created mathematical formulas. To record their findings, they learned to write on *papyrus*. To sail on the Nile, they designed boats.

Ancient Egypt's success as a civilization can also be attributed to the deserts that surrounded it. Because crossing these deserts was difficult, Egypt was relatively free from attack by other groups of people. Long periods of peace gave the Egyptians time to concentrate on building their society and their pyramids.

The Egyptians may have been the first people to make wine and brew beer.

This ancient Egyptian boat was
intended to provide transportation
for the pharaoh after death.

chapter 2
Building the Pyramids

The pyramids of Giza were built
about 4,500 years ago.

The Egyptian pyramids were built as tombs for *pharaohs*—Egypt's rulers—and other nobles. King Zoser's step pyramid, was built about 4,500 years ago. It was the first large building ever constructed entirely of stone. The Great Pyramid of Khufu is the largest pyramid ever built. Its base is as large as ten football fields. Each of the 2,250,000 stone blocks used to build the pyramid weighs close to 5,000 pounds (2,300 kg).

Zoser's pyramid, which is also called the Step Pyramid, was the first pyramid ever built.

It's hard to imagine how anyone could construct something as large as a pyramid, even in modern times. And yet the Egyptians did it with just four simple tools-the lever, the inclined plane, the wedge, and the pulley.

Preparing the Building Site

Before construction could begin, workers cleared sand and gravel away from the chosen site until they reached the desert's solid-rock floor. The ground had to be perfectly level—even a slight difference in height between one side of the pyramid and another could cause the entire structure to come crashing down.

Workers used A-shaped tools to make sure the ground was level.

To make sure the ground was level, the Egyptians may have used a wooden frame shaped like an A. By marking the center of the crossbar and hanging a weighted cord from the top of the A, the builders could determine whether a surface was perfectly level.

The builders may have also dug ditches crisscrossing the base area and then filled them with water. Since free-flowing water always forms a flat surface, the workers knew that the waterline was perfectly level.

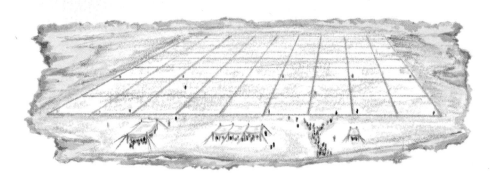

Crisscross channels were built across the pyramid site and filled with water. The waterline was used to determine whether the ground was level.

After draining the ditches, laborers cut the ground down to the water-lines and filled the ditches with rubble.

Meanwhile, architects were drawing plans on clay tablets. A pyramid appears to be a solid mass of stone, but it actually contains a number of tunnels and rooms as well as a passage from the outside. One room will house the pharaoh's *sarcophagus*, or coffin. Some pyramids also have rooms for the pharaoh's relatives and possessions. To confuse robbers, many pyramids have false tunnels and empty rooms.

All mummies were placed inside a sarcophagus.

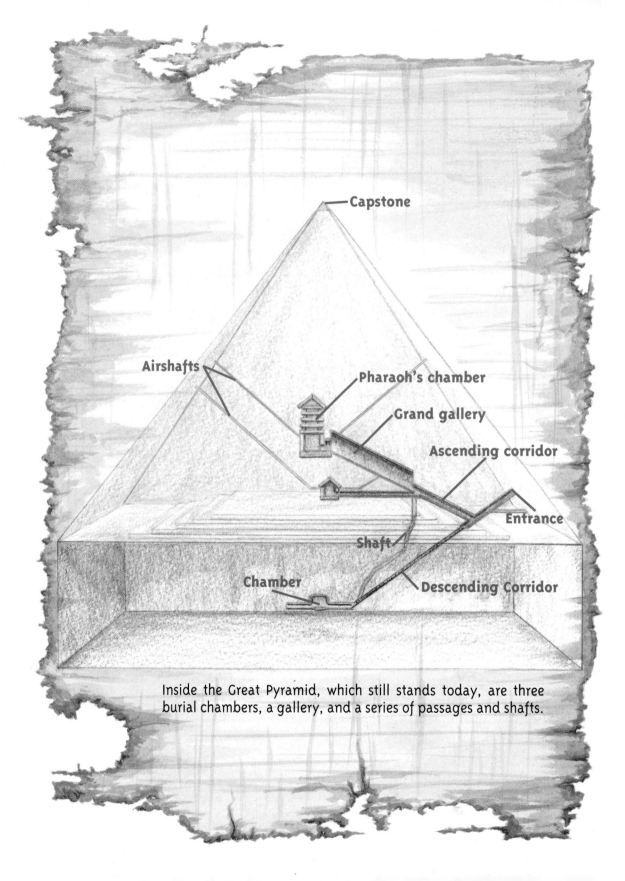

Capstone

Airshafts

Pharaoh's chamber

Grand gallery

Ascending corridor

Entrance

Shaft

Chamber

Descending Corridor

Inside the Great Pyramid, which still stands today, are three
burial chambers, a gallery, and a series of passages and shafts.

The ramp between the steps inside this pyramid corridor was used to slide the pharaoh's sarcophagus to its final resting place.

To make the pyramid's underground rooms and tunnels, the workers probably worked with *caissons*—large hollow tubes made of brick and stone. Each caisson was placed at the entrance of a tunnel and pushed forward while the workers inside removed dirt and rock from the caisson's path. The caisson's strong walls kept the tunnel from caving in. Laborers following behind the caisson reinforced the sides of the tunnel with stone. Caissons are still used to construct tunnels today.

The rock used to build pyramids came from quarries. After each stone was marked and cut, workers raised it onto a wooden sled and pulled it to the Nile. The blocks were loaded onto flat-bottomed boats and transported to the building site.

At the Quarry

The outer surfaces of the pyramids were covered with pure white limestone. The inner rooms were usually made of granite, a harder stone. Both types of rock came from quarries on the east side of the Nile. Metal chisels and saws, wooden mallets and wedges, and stone hammers strapped to wooden handles were the only tools Egyptian workers had to cut the millions of stone blocks needed to build each pyramid.

Before they began cutting the rock, the workers drew marks to outline each block. Then with chisels and mallets they chipped small cracks into the stone. Next, the workers hammered wooden wedges into the cracks and soaked the area with water. As the water was absorbed by the dry wood, the wedges swelled and split the limestone rock. The Egyptians may have also heated the cracks and then cooled them suddenly with water. The fast temperature change split the rock.

Once the gigantic blocks were cut, they had to be transported to the building site. To raise each block, the workers probably tied ropes of palm fiber around it and then tilted one side with a lever. The Egyptians may also have used a *weight arm* made of heavy timber. This tool had a central post and two arms, one short and one long. Workers slipped a sling under each block and then attached the sling to the tool's short arm. Small rocks placed on the long arm balanced the weight of the block. When the long arm was tipped, the block rose.

As soon as the massive block was lifted off the ground, a wooden sled was pushed underneath it. A team of workers pulled the sled out of the quarry along a path of logs—the logs kept the sled from sinking into the sand.

At the Building Site

As soon as the blocks were unloaded, masons cut them to the exact size needed for the pyramid. Workers cut away the larger bumps with saws or chisels and mallets. Then they smoothed the surface with rough stone or a piece of extremely hard rock.

Every surface of the block was tested with a *boning rod* to make sure it was perfectly level. The boning rod had three identical pegs, and a cord was attached to the tops of two pegs. Two workers rested these pegs on the stone and stretched the cord tightly. Another worker moved the third peg back and forth across the block's surface. If the surface was even, the third peg fit perfectly between the stone and the cord.

The workers used wooden right angles to make sure the corners were square. They knocked away extra rock with chisels or pieces of flint.

It must have taken days of backbreaking labor to make sure every block was exactly the right shape.

Finally, the workers dragged the stone blocks for the first layer into place. Ramps of mud and sand were built along the sides of the pyramids so that the blocks could be dragged to higher layers. Workers probably sprinkled water or oil over the stones to make them slide more easily. The blocks fit together so perfectly that no cement was needed. Not even a knife can be inserted between most blocks!

A surveyor checked that the corners of each layer were perfectly square. A *plumb line*—a cord attached to a pointed stone—was used to make sure that each layer rose at the correct angle. The cord was lowered until the stone just touched the earth. When it stopped swinging, it always made a right angle with the ground.

At the building site, the blocks were cut to the correct size and the surfaces were smoothed out. After making sure a block was perfectly square, workers dragged it up ramps of mud and sand. The block was then pushed into position.

The Egyptians placed a *capstone*—a pointed stone with a plug on the bottom—at the very top of every pyramid. The plug fit into a hole in the layer underneath. Once the capstone was in place, stoneworkers polished the outside of the pyramid. As they moved down toward the base, other workers removed the dirt ramps.

Thousands of years after they were built, Egypt's pyramids are still standing. Modern engineers and architects are amazed and fascinated by these monumental structures.

The inside walls of many tombs were covered with beautiful paintings.

The Pharaoh's Treasures

Pyramids contained treasures for the dead to use during their eternal life. Some tombs contain miniature statues of workers. The little figures— busy at tiny bakeries, butcher shops, and workrooms—were supposed to spare the dead from labor. Tomb paintings and a variety of *artifacts* provide important clues about the ancient Egyptians' lifestyle.

Limestone sculpture of a servant grinding grain

The pottery tells us that the Egyptians knew how to use a kiln to bake clay objects. The bricks reveal that the Egyptians knew how to sun-dry a mixture of mud and straw. (Our word "adobe" comes from the Egyptian word for brick.)

Tombs were also supplied with a variety of fine linen and wooden furniture. Egyptian women spun fibers of the flax plant into fine thread and wove it into cloth on flat looms shaped like bed frames. The weavers used sticks to pull the cross-threads. Carpenters built the wooden furniture with metal saws and hammers, chisels, and nails of copper or wood. They smoothed the wood with flat slabs of sandstone and sometimes glued expensive wood to cheaper material; this was the first *veneer*.

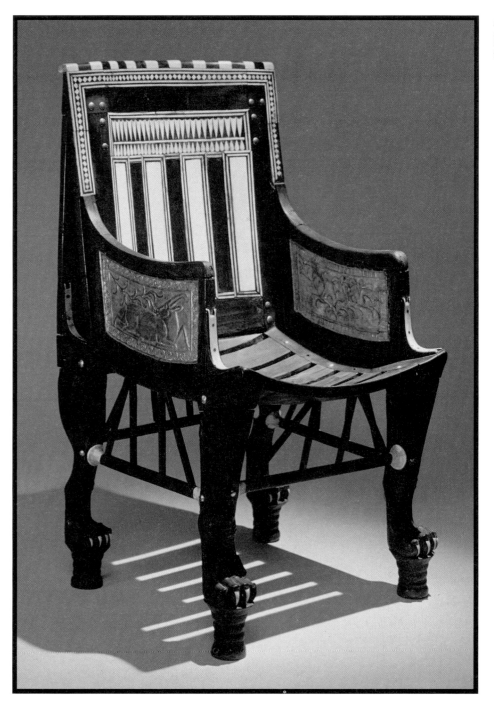

A chair recovered
from Tutankhamen's
tomb

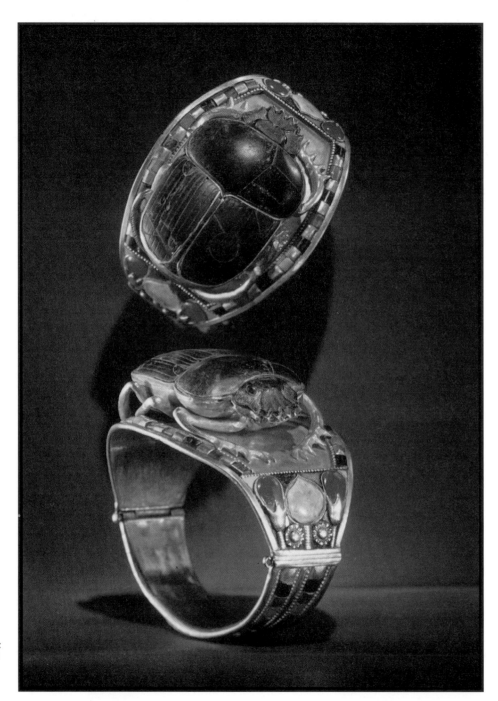

These bracelets were found in the tomb of the pharaoh Tutankhamen.

Pharaoh Khufu had two full-sized boats in his tomb. The Egyptians were skilled boat-builders, and created the earliest known sail. Boats were made of reeds lashed together and, later, of wood. The Egyptians dug one of the first canals to bypass rapids, so they could sail farther up the Nile and obtain treasures for themselves and for their eternal tombs.

The Egyptians were fine glassmakers. They did not know how to blow glass, but they shaped it by twisting thin rods. They also filled bags with sand and dipped them into melted glass. When the glass hardened, the bags of sand were removed.

Egyptians fashioned jewelry from glass, metal, and *faience*—a material made from powdered stone. The Egyptians knew how to make bronze—a mixture of copper and tin—and they molded silver and gold into various shapes. A dagger made of iron from a meteorite was discovered in Pharaoh Tutankhamen's tomb.

chapter 3
Early Egyptian Mathematics

Egyptians used math to keep track
of how much grain they produced.

About 3,500 years ago, Ahmes the Moonborn wrote a book called *How to Obtain Information About All Things Mysterious and Dark.* The "mysterious and dark" subject matter was mathematics. Ahmes' book explained how to multiply and divide fractions and how to calculate the area of a circle, square, and triangle or the volume of some solids.

Although this arithmetic would be simple for most of today's fifth-graders, it was a great discovery to most Egyptians. The little math they did know was usually related to their jobs. Surveyors, for example, could measure a right angle, and traders could add the weights and values of their goods.

Mathematical theory was studied only by people who held high positions in Egyptian society. Government officials needed to know math to calculate taxes and keep track of land ownership. Priests used it to predict the actions of the Nile god Hapi.

As far back as 5,000 years ago, the Egyptians could predict how the Nile's flood would

A representation of Hapi, the god of the Nile

Nilometers, such as this one in Cairo, are used to record the Nile's yearly flood.

affect them. Using *nilometers*, stone gauges with lines to measure how much the river rose, the priests could determine whether there would be a good harvest. They always hoped for a nilometer reading of about 25 feet (7.6 m), which meant the Nile would bring just enough water for the crops. A higher water level meant dangerous flooding, and a lower mark on the nilometer meant a poor harvest.

Counting

Mathematics depends on a system of counting. Early Egyptians probably chipped notches on wood or stone to record the passing of time. Later, symbols were created to stand for different numbers. Like most number systems, the Egyptian method of counting gave special importance to the number ten and multiples of ten, probably because people have ten fingers.

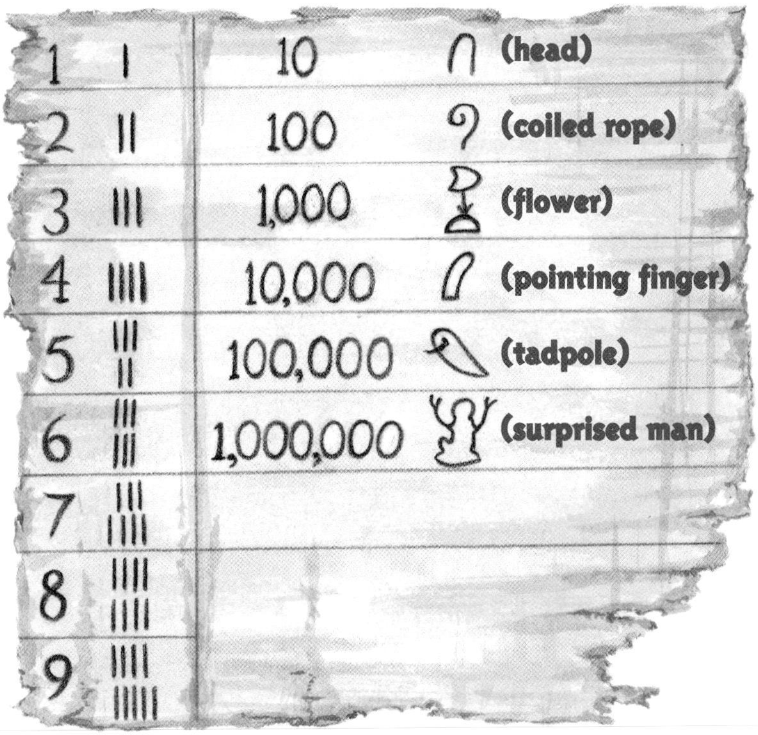

1	I	10	∩	(head)
2	II	100	?	(coiled rope)
3	III	1,000	⚘	(flower)
4	IIII	10,000	⌒	(pointing finger)
5	III II	100,000	⌢	(tadpole)
6	III III	1,000,000	�	(surprised man)
7	III IIII			
8	IIII IIII			
9	IIII IIIII			

In the counting system we use today, the position of the number, or *place value*, is very important. To us, the *3* in *321* means three hundreds, while the *3* in *123* means three units. Place value didn't matter to the Egyptians because they used different symbols for hundreds, tens, and units. They had no symbol for zero, although a blank space was occasionally used to represent the lack of a number. This is how the ancient Egyptians wrote 1,492:

Without place value, arithmetic is very complicated. When we add 765 and 321, for example, we add the numbers one column at a time—5 + 1, 6 + 2, and 7 + 3—to arrive at 1,086. The Egyptians' numerical symbols could not be broken down into smaller values that were easier to handle.

The Egyptians understood only fractions that were "one part of" the whole, and had a special symbol that meant "one part of." Values like $\frac{1}{7}$ and $\frac{1}{10}$ made sense to them, but $\frac{3}{7}$, $\frac{6}{7}$, and $\frac{9}{10}$ did not. The only way they knew how to write three-sevenths was $\frac{1}{7} + \frac{1}{7} + \frac{1}{7}$ or $\frac{1}{4} + \frac{1}{7} + \frac{1}{28}$.

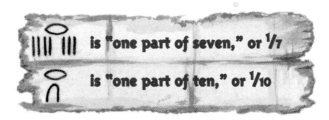

is "one part of seven," or $\frac{1}{7}$

is "one part of ten," or $\frac{1}{10}$

Measuring

The earliest Egyptian system of measurements was based on the body of the pharaoh. A *cubit* was the length of his forearm—from the elbow to the tip of his middle finger. The width of his palm and the width of four fingers held together were also used.

When measuring grain, the Egyptians used symbols based on the eye of the god Horus. A surveyor would draw Horus's eyebrow to represent the fraction $\frac{1}{8}$ or the eyeball to represent $\frac{1}{4}$.

The problem with this system was that all human bodies are different. Some people have fatter fingers, bigger hands, and longer arms than other people. The Egyptians soon realized that they needed a standard measurement system.

Official measuring sticks were created, although the old body-part names were kept. For example 1 cubit equaled 7 palms, and 1 palm equaled 4 digits (fingers). In the measuring systems we use today, 1 yard equals 3 feet and 1 foot equals 12 inches, 1 meter equals 10 centimeters and 1 centimeter equals 10 millimeters.

Egyptians created a system of weights based on a single grain of wheat. Later, standard stone weights were used.

Arithmetic

The Egyptians knew how to add and subtract. They could also multiply and divide, but their methods were very different from ours. To multiply 23 by 13, for example, the Egyptians made two columns of numbers. The first column always began with 1, and the second began with the number to be multiplied (in this case 23). Each line of the columns doubled the line before:

1	23
2	46
4	92
8	184.

Next, the Egyptians chose numbers from the first column that added up to the multiplier:

$$1 + 4 + 8 = 13.$$

Lastly, they added each number's partner:

$$23 + 92 + 184 = 299.$$

In other words, they added 1 × 23, 4 × 23, and 8 × 23. The answer was 13 × 23, or 299.

Division was also done with columns. To divide 48 by 8, for example, the columns began with 1 and 8 and doubled on each line:

1	8
2	16
4	32
8	64.

By trial and error the Egyptians would add the numbers in the second column to find numbers that totaled 48. In this case, 16 + 32 = 48. The answer to the division problem is the sum of their partners, 2 + 4, or 6. In effect, the Egyptians were calculating the answer to 16 ÷ 8 and 32 ÷ 8. If the two numbers in the second column could not be added to total the number being divided, the numbers that gave the closest total were used and the remainders were written as fractions.

Area, Angles, and Algebra

Because the Nile wiped out the boundary markers of each farmer's fields every year, surveyors had to be able to redraw the property lines. Surveyors, also called "rope stretchers," probably worked with a set of knotted ropes. For simple measurements, the surveyors laid out ropes in a straight line. Early on, the Egyptians discovered that a triangle measuring 3, 4, 5 or 5, 12, 13 would always include a right angle. By sighting with a right angle and constructing an imaginary triangle, surveyors could determine distances.

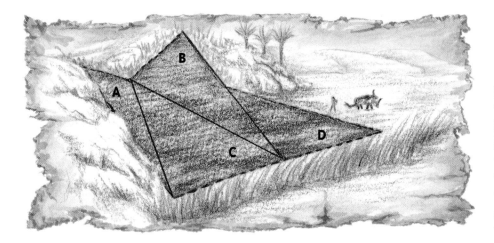

Egyptians measured the area of irregularly shaped fields by dividing it into triangles, finding the area of each triangle, and then adding all the areas together.

The amount of taxes a landowner paid was based on the area of each field, so government officials became skilled at computing the area of squares, rectangles, triangles, and circles. Most fields did not fit these shapes exactly, so irregular fields were divided into triangles. The area of the field in the figure above could be calculated by adding together the area of the triangles labeled A, B, C, and D.

The Egyptians even knew some basic *algebra*, a type of math you will probably learn in high school. In algebra, problems are often written in the form of *equations*, in which letters of the alphabet represent the unknown quantities. The goal of algebra is to figure out what number the letter stands for. For example, in the equation $2 \times x = 12$, the goal is to find out what number x stands for. In this case, x stands for the number 6 because $2 \times 6 = 12$.

Evidence for the development of algebra was found in an Egyptian document copied by Ahmes the Moonborn about 3,600 years ago. *Archaeologists* have also found ancient Egyptian scrolls containing problems with some unknown numbers.

chapter 4
Astronomy and Time

The Egyptians' earliest calendar was based on the phases of the moon.

Early Egyptians probably measured time by the most obvious change in their lives—the flooding of the Nile. Before long, however, they turned to *astronomy*, the study of objects outside Earth's atmosphere.

The brightest object in our night sky is the moon. In just $29\frac{1}{2}$ days the moon grows until it is a full round circle and then shrinks until it disappears completely. Each time a "new" moon appeared, the Egyptians began a new month. Twelve months were counted as 1 year. An Egyptian moon-year had 354 days. After several years, however, the Egyptians noticed that the Nile did not always flood during the same month. They could not use their calendar to predict accurately when the annual flood would occur.

The Egyptians solved this problem about 2,300 years ago. They noticed that Sirius, the brightest star in the sky, acted strangely. Every once in a while, the star vanished. When it reappeared, it was visible for just a few minutes at dawn. After that, Sirius stayed in the sky for a longer period of time each day, until it disappeared again. And Sirius always returned just before the Nile flooded.

Observing Sirius's movements allowed the Egyptians to predict the flooding of the Nile and prepare for the planting season. So the Egyptians made a new calendar based on Sirius. It was a good choice because Sirius' cycle is $36\frac{1}{4}$ days long—exactly the length of a year. (The length of a year is actually determined by the amount of time it takes Earth to revolve once around the sun.) With this new calendar, each month always came during the same season of the year.

The Egyptians subdivided their year into 12 months, each with 30 days, for a total of 360 days. So what happened to the other 5¼ days? The 5 days were added in as holidays and their origin was explained by a myth. According to this legend, the god Thoth had played a dice game with the moon and won some of its light. Thoth had then fashioned this light into the 5 extra days. This brought the yearly total to 365 days. Even though the Egyptian calendar was still one-fourth of a day short, it was the most accurate calendar in the ancient world.

The Egyptians also charted the movement of other stars across the sky. (Of course it is Earth that moves, not the stars, but this fact was not discovered until thousands of years later.) Egyptian astronomers tracked thirty-six specially chosen stars, called the "Indestructibles," with a forked stick and an attached cord. When the cord hung at a right angle to the ground, the astronomer could sight the stars through the forked stick and record their changing positions. The Egyptians eventually named the weeks of their calendar after the "Indestructibles."

The Egyptian astronomers grouped some stars into constellations named after familiar animals like crocodiles, oxen,

According to an Egyptian myth, Thoth, the god of wisdom and writing, won some of the moon's light in a dice game.

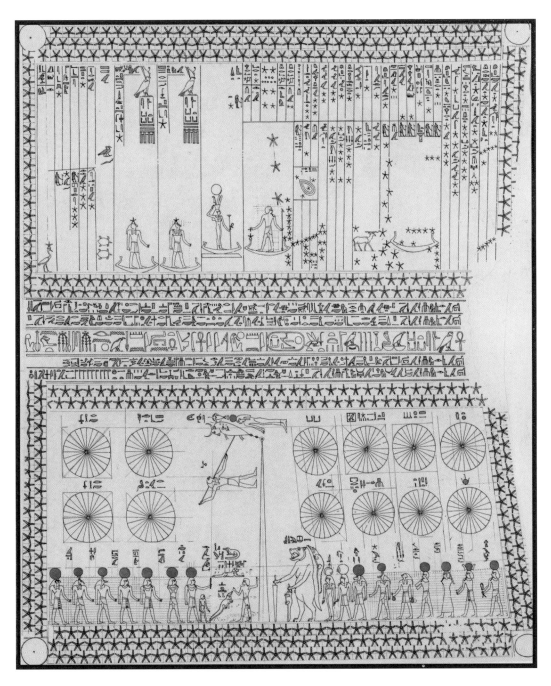

This painting on the ceiling of a
tomb includes information about the
movement of the stars and planets.

The Temple of Amon was completed during the rule of Ramses II.

and hippos. A group of stars that seemed to revolve around the North Pole and never set were called "The Imperishables." The Egyptians also observed Jupiter, Saturn, Venus, Mars, and perhaps Mercury. These planets were called "The Unwearied."

Astronomy and Architecture

The four sides of a pyramid always faced exactly north, south, east, and west. How did the architects manage to position the pyramids so precisely? It is possible that, before construction began, the architects built a tall circle of stone at the center of the site and asked a priest to mark the positions where a specific star rose in the evening and set in the morning. Halfway between these two marks was true north.

The ancient builders also positioned other structures according to the heavens. The Temple of Amon at Karnak has a long line of columns. An observer looking along this line at dawn on Midsummer Day will see the rising sun directly between the last two columns. At the pyramid of Khufu, the North Star can be sighted through an airshaft.

The Egyptians could also determine direction using the sun. They knew that the sun rises in the southeast in winter and in the northeast in summer. They marked the direction of the rising sun on Midsummer Day and Midwinter Day—the halfway point of each season. By halving the angle formed by these two lines, they found due east. A simpler, but less exact method, involved building a tall column. At noon, the shadow of the column points north. East and west can be found by crossing the shadow with a right-angle line.

Clocks and Timekeeping

The sun's shadow was also used to mark the passage of hours. The Egyptians' shadow clock had one flat arm and one upright arm. The upright arm was positioned to face due east at dawn. The upright arm cast a shadow on the flat arm. The longest shadow marked the sixth hour before noon; the shortest shadow marked midday. At that time, the clock was turned around. As the afternoon progressed, the shadow grew longer and longer.

The Egyptians also used water clocks. The simplest one was just a large bowl with a hole in the bottom. As the water flowed out of the bowl, hour lines became visible on the side of the bowl. The lines had to be carefully placed to allow for sloping sides of the bowl and the change in flow rate as the bowl empties. (A bowl filled to the top leaks more quickly than a bowl that is almost empty.) Another type of water clock counted hours as the water flowed into the bowl.

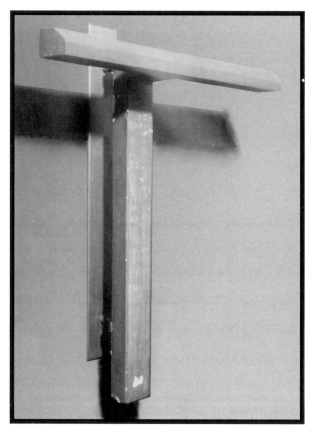

This shadow clock was used by Egyptians who lived more than 3,000 years ago.

A water clock recovered from the Karnak Temple

Egyptian hours were made by dividing both day and night into twelve equal parts. The length of a day changes with the seasons, and so does the length of one-twelfth of a day. In winter, days are shorter than in summer. As a result, the twelve winter-day hours were shorter than the twelve summer-day hours. The opposite is true of winter-night hours. Water clocks had markings for both summer and winter. The winter night was fourteen fingers of water tall, while the summer night was only twelve fingers tall.

chapter 5

Ancient Egyptian Medicine

Ancient Egyptians ground leaves, stems, and roots to make remedies for a variety of illnesses.

When you are sick, you might visit a family doctor or a specialist. A pharaoh had the same choice. Among his doctors were the "Palace Eye Physician" and the "Palace Stomach-Bowel Physician." Chances are the pharaoh received good care—the Egyptians had the best medical knowledge in the ancient world.

Making a Mummy

The Egyptians believed that a preserved body could go on to another world with the spirit of the dead person. This religious idea may have inspired the Egyptians to *mummify* bodies—to preserve them forever.

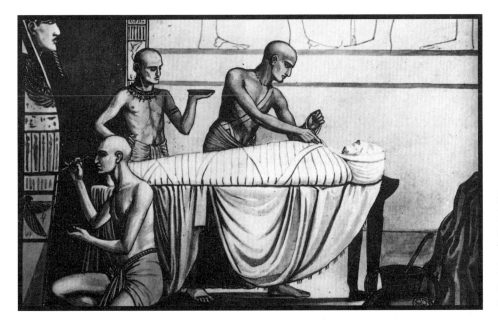

Embalmers required 70 days to prepare a body for burial. They chanted prayers and spells as they wrapped each body.

Bronze knives like this one were used by Egyptian embalmers.

Because dry material is less likely to decay, the Egyptians removed as much water as possible from the body. First, a priest removed the heart, liver, and other organs. The body cavity and organs were washed with wine. (The alcohol in the wine is a natural germ killer.) The body and its organs were packed in natron (a type of salt) for 2 months and then treated with resin (a sealant) and wax. The organs were placed in jars and the body was wrapped in linen. Despite this careful process, however, the dry Egyptian air was what actually made mummification possible.

After a person's internal organs were removed, they were stored in canopic jars.

This engraving, which shows two men making an herbal remedy, is about 5,000 years old.

Early Druggists

Modern parents sometimes give castor oil to their children as a cure for an upset stomach. Thousand of years ago the Egyptians chewed castor berries for the same ailment. These berries were just one remedy in the ancient Egyptian "medicine cabinet." Drugs were also made from many other plants and spices such as anise, cumin, and poppy flowers. The Egyptians even made medicines of copper, sodium bicarbonate, and other minerals. Parts or all of various animals—birds, pigs, crocodiles, and ants—were also prescribed. Creams and ointments were created with goose grease, honey, or animal fat.

Poppies were used in a number of Egyptian remedies.

How effective were these remedies? Some were better than others. Patients with night blindness were probably helped by eating the liver their doctor prescribed. However, the treatment for nearsightedness (honey, lead, and water from a pig's eye injected into the patient's ear) was useless. Still, the Egyptians did discover a remarkable number of drugs.

Cranky babies were given pods of the poppy plant mixed with "fly dirt which is on the wall." Poppies supply opium, a calming drug. Hartshorn (powdered deer antler) was used to treat many ailments. Today doctors prescribe spirits of hartshorn—an ammonia mixture—for several conditions. Earaches were treated with a mixture of salt and hot wine. Today, eardrops contain alcohol and boric powder. The Egyptians also used acacia and honey as a form of birth control. When mixed, these two substances form lactic acid, an ingredient in some modern birth control products.

The First Medical Books

While mummification taught the Egyptians about the structure of the body's internal organs, the Egyptians also learned about medicine from the living. They noted symptoms and experimented with drugs and treatments. Successful healing methods were taught to new generations of doctors, often by means of papyrus scrolls. These were the world's first medical textbooks.

One ancient Egyptian scroll lists heart conditions and another discusses diseases of women and children. A "first aid" scroll explains how to treat a variety of injuries, and "recipe scrolls" give directions for making medicines. On a scroll, referred to as *The Book of Surgery*, forty-eight medical conditions are listed by body part from the head down. This scroll, which

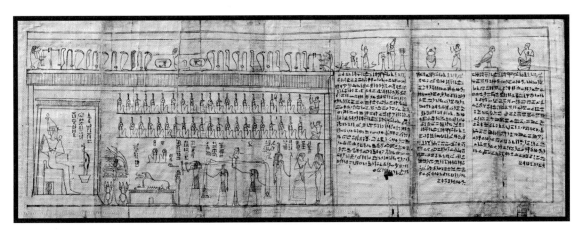

Egyptian doctors kept track of remedies and procedures on papyrus scrolls. Many of these scrolls still exist today.

is about 3,550 years old, is actually a copy of another document written almost 1,000 years earlier.

The Book of Surgery includes instructions for examination and diagnosis of a wide variety of medical conditions. According to the scroll, some conditions are considered treatable and others as "not to be treated" because they are hopeless. In the case of a wound above the eyebrow, the doctor is directed to stitch the wound and place fresh meat on it. After the first day, a mixture of grease and honey is the prescribed treatment.

Egyptian doctors knew how to set broken bones. They sawed through the skull with copper tools to treat head wounds and opened the skin with straight knives similar to modern scalpels. They were among the first to use bandages and compresses. They also used several types of forceps, or grasping tools. They expected cuts to become infected (they had no antibiotics), but knew that they could tie the edges of a wound together to reduce scarring. One scroll even discusses skin grafts—transferring skin from one part of the body to another.

Hesi Re, a high official, is shown here holding a staff and scepter, which were considered symbols of authority.

Dentistry

Hesi Re, who lived about 4,600 years ago, was one of the world's first dentists. As the "Chief of Toothers and Physicians," he was probably a very busy man. Judging from mummies recovered from tombs, the teeth of ancient Egyptians were often infected or worn down to the gum line. This damage may have been caused by sand and dirt in the food they ate.

Most Egyptians ground their grain between stones and kept it in open storage bins where it probably picked up sand and dirt.

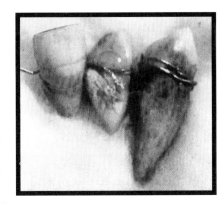

The first known set of "false" teeth

Luckily, the Egyptians knew how to fill cavities and treat infections. Archeologists have found a 3,800-year-old Egyptian jawbone with a hole under a molar. The jaw was probably pierced so that the pus from a dental infection could drain out. A 4,500-year-old Egyptian skull has the earliest known set of false teeth. Held together by gold wire, the false teeth appear to have been anchored to a hole drilled in another tooth.

Medical Mistakes

While Egyptian doctors could identify many of the body's organs, they did not always realize how the parts worked in living people. During mummification, for example, the brain was discarded because it was considered

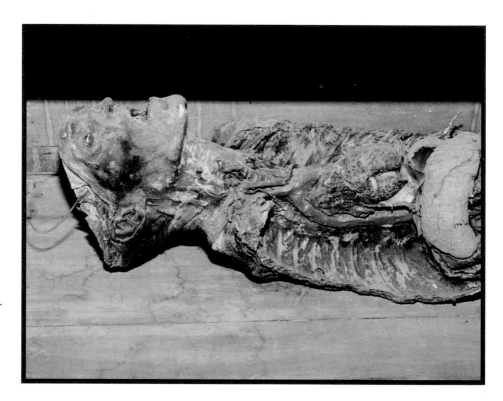

During mummification, the corpse's skull was sawed in half, so the brain could be removed.

unimportant. Although the Egyptians knew that the pulse and heartbeat were related, they had only one word for muscles and blood vessels and believed that both were responsible for movement. They also thought that blood vessels carried many different substances—air, water, blood, semen, urine, and solid wastes.

The Egyptians mixed science, religion, and magic when they practiced medicine. A doctor would often recite spells over a clay statue, draw magic circles, or prescribe spells. Certain words had to be recited every few hours—just like doses of medicine! Many were prayers to the goddess Isis, who had once healed the god Osiris.

Sometimes doctors prescribed chants to encourage positive thinking. Someone with eye disease, for example, might say, "The crocodile is weak and powerless." According to Egyptian myth, the crocodile stole the eye of the sun. At other times the disease itself was addressed. A spell for the common cold told the "poison nose" and "son of poison nose" to flow out and begone. It's no wonder ancient Egyptians had no luck treating colds—modern medical science can't cure them either!

The ancient Egyptian goddess Isis, seated on a throne

chapter 6
What Ancient Egypt Gave Us

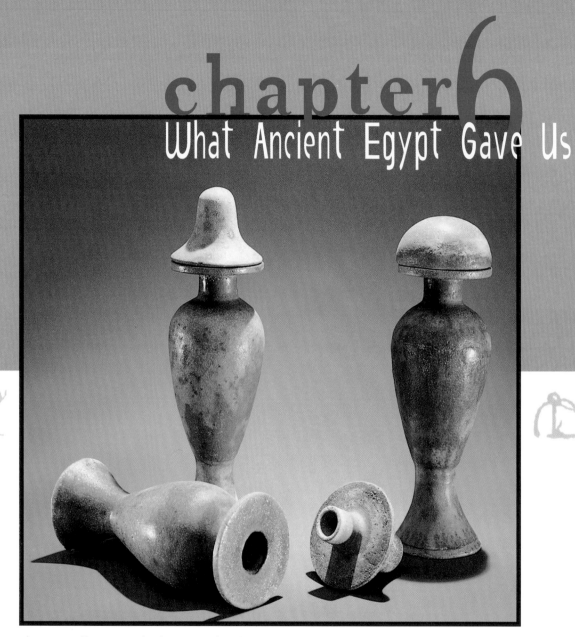

These small vases, which are made
of glass and faience, were found in
the tomb of Tutankhamen.

In Egypt the past is alive. The majestic pyramids are survivors of ancient times, as is the simple shaduf a farmer dips for water and the mud bricks that villagers set to bake in the sun. It is still possible to find flat looms, sun clocks, papyrus, and faience made in the 5,000-year-old way. These are only the obvious traces of the past. Many other achievements of the early Egyptians also appear in our modern world.

What is the most important contribution ancient Egypt has made to modern times? It may be time itself. Our sun-based calendar came to us from Egypt by way of Julius Caesar, who brought it to Rome about 2,050 years ago. So did our 24-hour days, although our winter and summer hours are always the same length.

The Egyptians also laid the foundations of geometry, a type of advanced math, with their formulas for calculating area and volume and their study of angles. Their practical engineering math was passed along to the Greeks when Alexander the Great conquered Egypt about 2,330 years ago. The Greeks extended this knowledge into the theories of math taught to schoolchildren today.

The scientific study of medicine also began in ancient Egypt. Their physicians handed down knowledge of anatomy, drugs, and surgery to later cultures. They also passed along an attitude. The ancient doctors were taught to observe, examine, diagnose, and prescribe treatment, just as doctors do today.

This detail of an Egyptian tomb painting shows a farmer plowing a field with oxen.

As pioneers in irrigation and agriculture, the ancient Egyptians were the first to build canals and reservoirs, to use a plow, to keep cattle, sheep, oxen, goats, and donkeys.

The form and craftsmanship of the pyramids probably inspired architects of later eras. The Egyptians invented many techniques for handling stone, and they were the first to use it in monumental structures. Until the Egyptians worked with this material, no one else in the world had even laid a slab of stone on top of two columns.

Recently an underground tomb containing almost 100 rooms was discovered. It will take decades to explore the tomb completely, and no one knows what wonders will be found. Yet even if no scientific artifacts appear, the Egyptians' achievements stand out. Their ideas and tools have been passed down through more than 100 centuries to shape modern science and modern civilization.

GLOSSARY

algebra—a form of arithmetic in which letters represent numbers.

archaeologist—a scientist who studies past human life and activities.

artifact—an object remaining from an ancient civilization.

astronomy—the study of objects outside Earth's atmosphere.

boning rod—a tool with three pegs of equal height, two connected by a cord and one loose. It was used to level stone.

caisson—a large tube-shaped structure used to build tunnels.

capstone—a pointed stone with a plug on the bottom. A capstone was placed at the very top of each pyramid.

cubit—a measure of length originally equal to the distance between the pharaoh's elbow and the tip of his middle finger.

equation—in algebra, a problem using letters to represent unknown values.

faience—a material made from powdered stone. It was used to make jewelry.

mummify—to enbalm or preserve.

nilometer—a stone gauge with lines used to measure the floodwaters of the Nile.

papyrus—a paperlike material made from reeds.

pharaoh—an Egyptian king.

place value—the value given to a digit as a result of its position in a number. In 71, the place value of 7 is tens. In 718, the place value of 7 is hundreds.

plumb line—a simple tool that can be used to establish a true vertical.

quarry—an open excavation site where the materials such as stone are dug out for use in construction or industry.

sarcophagus—a pharaoh's coffin.

shaduf—a weighted pole used by ancient Egyptians to raise water.

silt—a type of soil that contains a large quantity of crumbled sedimentary rock and a little bit of clay.

veneer—a thin layer of expensive wood laid over cheaper wood to produce furniture or other wooden items at a lower cost.

weight arm—a tool used by ancient Egyptians to move huge stones for the pyramids.

RESOURCES

Books

Defrates, Joanna. *What Do We Know About Egypt?* New York: Peter Bedrick Books, 1991.

Green, Robert. *Tutankhamun.* Danbury, CT: Franklin Watts, 1996.

Hart, George. *Ancient Egypt.* New York: Time-Life, The Nature Company Discovery Library, 1995.

Jessop, Joanne. *The X-Ray Picture Book of Big Buildings of the Ancient World.* London: Watts, 1992.

Kerr, Daisy. *Ancient Egyptians.* Danbury, CT: Franklin Watts, 1996.

Kondeatis, Christos and Sara Mitland. *Ancient Egypt Pack.* Boston: Bulfinch, Little Brown and Company, 1996.

Morley, Jacqueline. *How Would You Survive as an Ancient Egyptian?* New York: Franklin Watts, 1995.

Putnam, James. *Pyramid.* New York: Eyewitness, Knopf, 1994.

Tiano, Oliver. *Ramses II and Egypt.* New York: Henry Holt, 1995.

Internet Sites

Due to the changeable nature of the Internet, sites appear and disappear very quickly. The following resources offered useful information on ancient Egypt at the time of publication.

Welcome to Ancient Egypt provides information about the Sphynx, pyramids, the Nile, afterlife, hieroglyphics, Egyptian gods, and Tutankhamen. Its address is **http://www.geocities.com/Athens/Acropolis/3076/index.html**.

The Egyptian Museum is a great place to find out more about Egyptian mummies, sculptures, tomb equipment, written documents, and jewelry and other accessories. It can be reached at **http://www.idsc.gov.eg/culture/ egy-mvs.htm.**

Egyptology Resources is a site set up by the Newton Institute at the University of Cambridge. It has information about upcoming conferences, exhibitions, seminars, and articles as well as e-mail addresses of egyptologists. The site also has links to many other related home pages. It's address is **http://www.newton.cam.ac.uk/egypt/**.

Exploring Ancient World Culture includes maps, timelines, essays, and images that describe ancient civilizations in India, China, Greece, and the Near East. It can be reached at **http://eawc.evansville.edu/index.htm**.

INDEX

ABOUT THE AUTHOR

Geraldine Woods is the author of more than thirty-five books for young people, many written with her husband Harold. She teaches English and directs the independent study program at the Horace Mann School in New York City. The Woodses have one son, Thomas, who is now in law school. Ms. Woods frequently visits the Egyptian section of the Metropolitan Museum of Art.